YOU SHOULD MEET Misty Copeland

by Laurie Calkhoven
illustrated by Monique Dong

Ready-to-Read

Simon Spotlight
New York London Toronto Sydney New Delhi

CONTENTS

Introduction

Have you ever dreamed of being a ballerina? Have you wondered about the hard work that goes into twirling across a stage, or flying through the air in a giant leap? What if you looked different from all the ballerinas you'd ever seen, but you knew in your heart you should be one?

If you've ever wondered about those things, then you should meet Misty Copeland. Misty is the first African American woman to earn the position of principal dancer, the highest level a dancer can achieve, in the American Ballet Theatre. She has also inspired young people all over the world to go after their **dreams**.

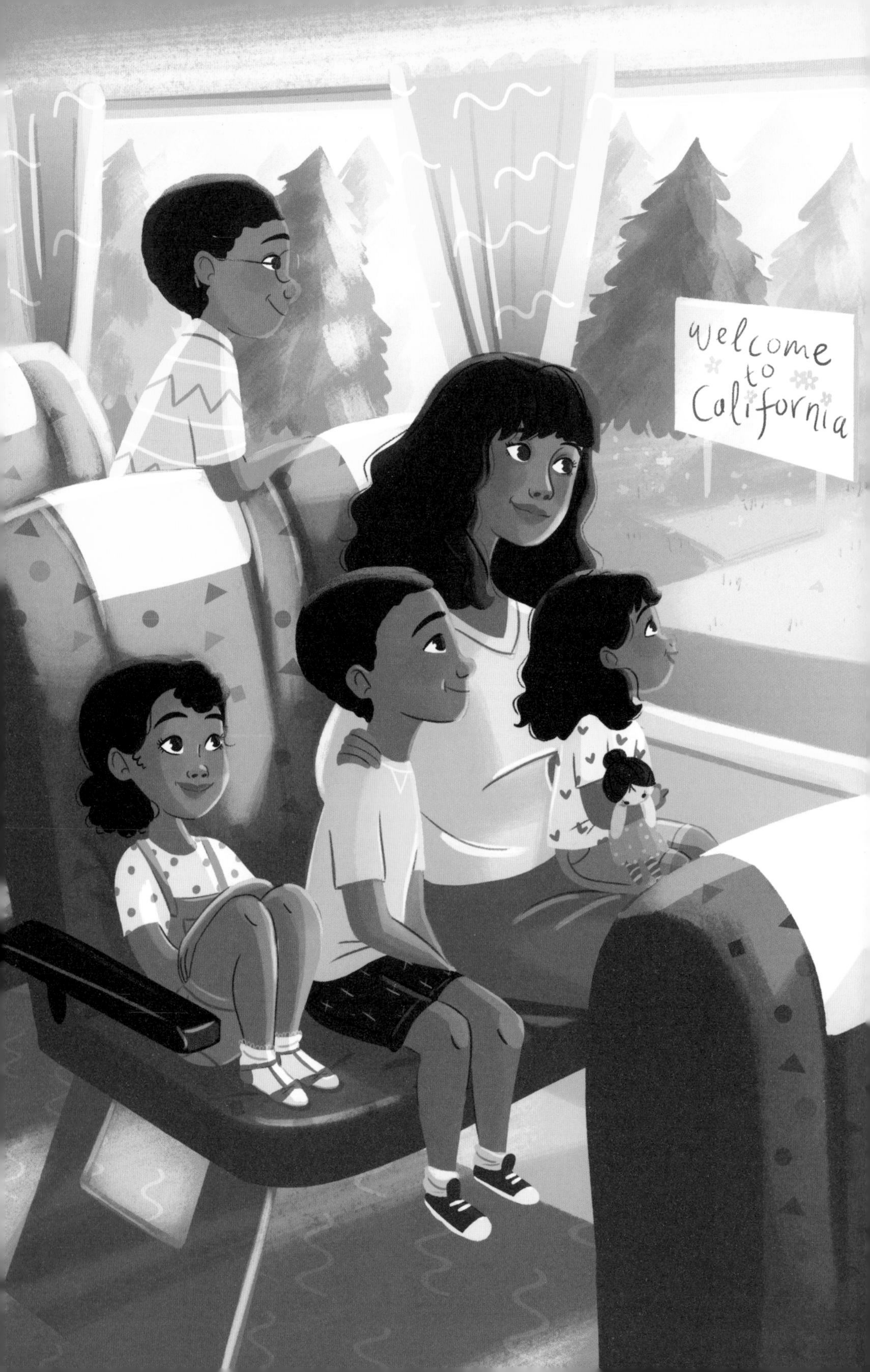
welcome to California

Chapter 1
Before Ballet

Misty was born on September 10, 1982, in Kansas City, Missouri. She had three older siblings, two brothers and a sister. When Misty was two, her mother left her father. The family took a bus across the United States to San Pedro, California. Misty wouldn't see her father again until she was grown up.

From then on, Misty was on the move. Her mother married and divorced two more times and had two more children. Each time her mother divorced, the family moved to a new house.

Misty enjoyed being part of a big family, but all the changes made her feel worried. She worried most about making mistakes at school. She made up for that by getting to school an hour early every morning. She studied and got good grades.

Life wasn't all school, though. Misty loved to watch gymnastics on television. She taught herself to do cartwheels, backbends, and other moves.

Dancing around the house to Mariah Carey's music videos also made Misty happy. When she was in middle school, she *choreographed* a dance (that means she created a sequence of steps and moves) for herself and her two best friends. They danced in the school talent show.

Misty loved being onstage. "I felt fierce," she later wrote in her autobiography.

Chapter 2
First Steps

Middle school brought Misty new challenges. She decided to try to win a place on the school's *drill team* like her sister, Erica, had done before her. A drill team performs dance moves for a school audience. Misty wanted to be more than just part of the team. She wanted to be the captain.

Misty created her own routine and danced her best. One night she got a phone call from the team's coach, Elizabeth Cantine. Misty was named captain of the drill team! She loved being team captain. Practice was one place where she didn't feel worried.

Coach Cantine had a background in
ballet. She taught Misty some ballet moves
for the drill team and saw how good Misty
was. She gave Misty the idea of taking a
ballet class at the local Boys & Girls Club.

The Boys & Girls Club was another place where Misty didn't feel worried. The Boys & Girls Club is a safe place where kids can go after school to play sports, be creative, and have fun. Misty and her brothers and sisters went to the local club almost every day after school.

Misty wanted to make her coach happy. Even though she knew nothing about ballet, she went to the class. She didn't have a leotard or tights or ballet shoes. For two weeks Misty sat and watched the ballet dancers. She was afraid she would look silly if she tried to dance. But one day she did try, wearing her gym clothes and dancing in her socks.

Most serious ballerinas start dancing by the time they are seven years old. Misty was thirteen when she started. Her ballet teacher, Cindy Bradley, saw Misty's talent from the very beginning. She knew right away that Misty was a special dancer. It wasn't long before Misty left the Boys & Girls Club to dance every day in Cindy's ballet studio.

Chapter 3
Becoming a Ballerina

Soon Misty started to feel like a ballerina. She took classes with dancers who had been training for years, and kept up with them. Within a few months she was dancing *en pointe*, or on the tips of her toes. It takes most dancers years to develop this skill. In just a few months Misty was dancing difficult steps and soaring past the other dancers.

At the same time, things were not good at home. Misty's second stepfather often said hurtful things to her mother and to her siblings. The family left him and moved into a small motel room next to a busy highway.

Misty got a ride to the ballet studio with Cindy after school every day, but she had to take a long bus ride home. By then ballet was more than a hobby for Misty. The world of ballet was a place where she felt safe and happy, a place where she was able to shine. The ballet classes were worth the hour-long bus ride home every night.

Misty's mother saw how hard her
daughter worked. She saw how tired
Misty was. She told Misty it was too much,
she'd have to give up ballet. Misty was
heartbroken. The next day she cried as
she told Cindy she couldn't come back to
class.

Cindy told Misty's mother that Misty had a chance to be a star. Cindy didn't want Misty to leave class. Together Cindy and Misty's mother decided that Misty would live with Cindy during the week to be closer to school and at the motel with her family on weekends.

Misty's weekends were often busy with performances. She spent less and less time with her family. After almost three years Misty's mother told Misty that it was time to come home.

Both Misty's mother and Cindy thought they knew what was best for Misty. Misty's mother wanted her to move back home. Cindy wanted Misty to continue to live with her and to dance. The two women went to court and asked the court to decide where Misty should live. Misty was scared and sad. She wanted to make everyone happy.

Chapter 4
Misty Takes New York by Storm

The court decided that Misty would move back in with her family and take lessons at a new studio closer to home after school. After a few months her mother got a better job and they moved out of the motel. Misty soon settled into her new ballet studio, even though she missed her old friends and teachers.

Misty continued to learn in her new studio. The following year she was invited to a summer program at the American Ballet Theatre (ABT) in New York City. ABT is one of the best ballet companies in the world.

Misty had wanted to dance for ABT ever since she had seen Paloma Herrera dance with the ballet company in the 1990s. Paloma was one of the youngest stars in the history of ABT. She was fifteen when she moved from Argentina to New York to join the *corps de ballet*, the group of dancers in the background of ballet performances. Two years later she was promoted to soloist. When she was nineteen, Paloma became a principal dancer.

Misty knew that she had started dancing too late to become a principal dancer at nineteen, but she wanted to follow Paloma's path. If she made it to Paloma's level, she would be the first

African American woman to do so in the history of the American Ballet Theatre.

Now Misty was going to dance for the same ballet company in New York City. "I was ready to take the Big Apple by storm," Misty wrote in her autobiography. And she did. After she completed the summer program, ABT invited her to join them full-time.

It was a hard decision, but Misty decided to go home and finish her last year of high school. She hoped that ABT would make her the same offer the

following summer. And they did.

Misty became a member of the corps de ballet. She was the only African American woman out of eighty dancers. She worried that she would never fit in.

The days were long and hard. Misty took a ninety-minute ballet class every morning and then rehearsed for seven hours.

At night the dancers performed.

By the end of her first year, Misty was beginning to work her way up in the company. Then one day while she was dancing, pain exploded in her back. The stress of dancing had injured a bone in Misty's spine. For the next year she wore a back brace for twenty-three hours a day and couldn't dance.

During that year Misty's body changed. She became curvier than she had been before. Once she was able to dance again, she had to learn how to dance all over again in her new body. People began to tell her that she was too "athletic" to be a

ballerina. Her strong muscles stood out.

No one said that there wasn't a place in ballet for an African American woman, but Misty knew some people thought that. She just kept dancing and showed them how **graceful and strong** she was.

Six years after she joined the corps de ballet, Misty was named a *soloist*. A soloist is a performer with a special role in the ballet. It had been over twenty years since an African American woman had had that honor at American Ballet Theatre. The first African American women soloists had been Nora Kimball and Shelley Washington, who had joined the company as soloists in the 1980s. Now Misty's name was being added to that short list.

Chapter 5
Twirling into History

It wasn't long before Misty was standing out because of her incredible dancing. People outside the ballet world noticed her too.

Misty starred in a commercial for a sportswear company. In the commercial a little girl read a letter listing all the reasons why she could never be a ballerina, such as having the wrong body type for ballet, and at age thirteen she was too old to be considered. As the girl spoke, Misty twirled and leapt across the stage. Within one week, more than four million people had watched the commercial on the Internet.

The support of Misty's friends and fans helped her to keep doing the hard work to win the best roles in the ballet company. In the spring of 2012 Misty was picked for the lead role in *The Firebird*, a famous ballet. Misty was the first African American woman ever to dance the role for a major ballet company, and she earned rave reviews. But dancing had also caused another injury. Misty needed surgery to repair fractures in her leg.

Some doctors said she would never dance again. But Misty didn't give up. She worked hard and got better, and danced more roles, including the lead role in *Swan Lake*. The lead in *Swan Lake* is the role every ballerina imagines herself performing. Dancing this role was a dream come true.

Misty also wrote her autobiography, and a separate picture book called *Firebird*.

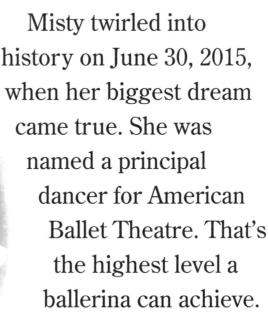

Misty twirled into history on June 30, 2015, when her biggest dream came true. She was named a principal dancer for American Ballet Theatre. That's the highest level a ballerina can achieve. Principal dancers almost always get the biggest roles in ballet. Their pictures are also published in the ballet programs, and young dancers all over the world look up to them. Misty is the first African American woman to be a principal dancer in ABT's history.

What's next for this unstoppable ballerina? Only time will tell, but it's clear that Misty will continue to inspire young people to go after their dreams. A few days after being named principal dancer, she said, "You can dream big, and it doesn't matter what you look like, where you come from, what your background is. That's the example that I want to set and what I want to leave behind."

Now that you've met Misty Copeland, wouldn't you agree that anything is possible?

Dream big!

BUT WAIT...

THERE'S MORE!

Turn the page to learn more about ballet.

Learn the finer *pointes* of the five basic positions!

Lesson number one for any ballet dancer is how to hold their arms and legs. Sounds easy, right? There are five basic positions, and all of them take years of practice to get just right. If you try these positions at home, be careful and don't attempt to force your toes to turn all the way out to the side! It takes dancers many years of training to get their hips turned out enough that their toes point to the side. You can injure yourself if you try to force your legs into an unnatural position.

In first position the dancer's heels are together and their toes are pointed outward. This outward positioning of the feet is called *turn-out*. When a dancer first begins learning ballet, their feet will form a V in first position. As they slowly progress, the opening of the V will widen until their feet form a straight line. It takes many years of training to safely achieve a 180-degree turn-out. In first position the arms are held in front of the dancer, either an inch or two from the thighs or out in front of the stomach. The fingers should almost touch, and the arms should be rounded, as if the dancer were holding a beach ball.

In second position the dancer's

heels are a few inches apart, and their toes are pointed outward. The arms are still slightly rounded but are held out to the sides.

In **third position** one foot is in front of the other. The heel of the front foot touches the arch, or middle of the back foot. The toes are pointed outward. One arm is raised above the head. The other arm is held out to the side. Third position for the feet is rarely used because it's so similar to fifth position, but third position for the arms is used regularly.

In **fourth position** one foot is a few inches in front of the other, and the toes are pointed outward. If the right foot is in front, the right arm is raised above the head and the left is held out in front.

In **fifth position** the feet are arranged the same as they are in third position, except the front foot covers the whole back foot. Both arms are slightly rounded and held above the head, with the fingers almost touching.

43

The History of Ballet

Ballet began as a party activity in fifteenth-century Italy, during the *Renaissance* (say: REN-nah-sance), a time when people in Europe were very interested in art and literature. The nobility and court wore fancy masks and danced for their guests. The steps were arranged by a dancing master.

Settings, costumes, and even poetry were added to ballet performances in sixteenth-century France with *ballet de cour* (court ballet). The dancers wore masks and long ball gowns, and the way they moved was very different from how modern-day ballerinas move.

King Louis XIV was the first to hire professional ballet dancers. He was a fan of the pastime and played many roles himself. When he couldn't dance anymore, he paid the best performers to entertain him. Suddenly, ballet became a career.

King Louis XIV

In the mid-1700s Jean-Georges Noverre had the idea to tell a story through movement, the way an opera told a story through song. He created *ballet d'action*, and the art form took to the stage.

In the mid-nineteenth century, ballets such as *Giselle* called for gently floating spirits and fairies. To create this illusion, ballerinas wore flowing skirts and skimmed the floor in newly invented pointe shoes.

The second half of the nineteenth century brought us *The Nutcracker*, *The Sleeping Beauty*, and *Swan Lake*. Ballerinas' flowing skirts became short tutus, and dancers showed off complex pointe work, high leg lifts, and the elegant movements we see today.

Ballet has continued to grow and change. George Balanchine's (say: bal-an-SHEEN) ballets expressed ideas without telling stories. Martha Graham pioneered modern dance. Alvin Ailey helped popularize modern dance and brought African American culture into the spotlight on ballet's biggest stages.

In addition to those we've mentioned, we can thank countless individuals for transforming ballet from a Renaissance pastime into a celebrated and soaring art.

Ballet by the Numbers

• Ballet dancers who aspire to dance professionally take up to 15 classes per week and usually begin training when they are 7 years old.

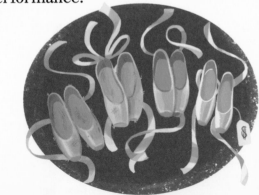

• A professional dancer (someone who earns a living by dancing) usually retires when he or she is 30 to 40 years old.

• An average professional ballerina can go through 6 pairs of pointe shoes a week and 1 pair per performance.

• A pair of pointe shoes costs about $50 to $80.

• The average ballerina trains for 8 to 10 years before becoming a professional.

• The average professional ballet dancer is practicing, rehearsing, and performing for 7 to 10 hours each day.

• American Ballet Theatre employed 18 principals, 13 soloists, and 57 corps de ballet dancers as of September 2015.

• In addition to the 5 basic positions, ballet dancers must learn the 8 positions of the body used in performances.

• One of the most famous ballet choreographers, George Balanchine, created 465 works in his lifetime.

Now that you've met Misty, what have you learned?

1. In what year was Misty born?

a. 1932   b. 1952   c. 1982

2. Misty's life has been "on the move" since she was two years old. What does that mean?

a. She has experienced many changes since then.

b. She started taking ballet lessons when she was two years old.

c. Since she learned to walk, she's had a hard time sitting still.

3. For how long did Misty train before she was dancing en pointe, or on the tips of her toes?

a. A few days   b. A few months   c. A year

4. When did Misty realize she wanted to dance for American Ballet Theatre?

a. When she moved to New York   b. When she saw Paloma Herrera perform

c. During her first ballet class

5. What did Misty mean when she said she was ready to "take the Big Apple by storm?"

a. She wanted to become a star in New York City.

b. She wanted to tour San Francisco as quickly as possible.

c. She wanted to fly over Manhattan.

6. When people said Misty was too "athletic" to be a ballerina, what did they mean?

a. She spent too much time at the gym instead of rehearsal.

b. She stood out because she was an awkward dancer.

c. She didn't look like a ballerina because her muscles stood out.

7. What was historical about Misty's being promoted to principal dancer at American Ballet Theatre?

a. She was the first African American dancer admitted to the company.

b. She was the first African American woman to be made principal dancer at the company.

c. She had the greatest number of injuries of any American Ballet Theatre principal dancer.

8. Misty says she wants to set an example. What is that example?

a. Practice makes perfect.   b. A ballerina can achieve anything.

c. You can dream big no matter what your background is.

Answers: 1. c   2. a   3. b   4. b   5. a   6. c   7. b   8. c

YOU SHOULD MEET

Lin-Manuel Miranda

by Laurie Calkhoven

illustrated by Alyssa Petersen

Ready-to-Read

Simon Spotlight

New York   London   Toronto   Sydney   New Delhi

CONTENTS

Introduction

Have you ever dreamed about writing songs? Or about singing on the Broadway stage? How about making movies? Maybe you enjoy watching and listening to other people act and sing. Or maybe you want to spend your life singing and dancing and making people happy.

If you like to do any of those things, you should meet Lin-Manuel Miranda.

Lin-Manuel wrote *Hamilton*, one of the most popular Broadway musicals of all time. He also inspired people all over the world to learn about the beginnings of the United States of America. He taught the world about Latin music and Latino traditions. And he didn't do it overnight or by himself. Lin-Manuel spent many years working on his music and learning his craft. He also had a strong team of friends who helped him.

Lin-Manuel made his dreams come true. Once you meet him, no matter what you dream of doing, you'll be inspired to make your dreams come true too.

Chapter 1
New York Dreams

Lin-Manuel Miranda was born on January 16, 1980, in New York City. His parents, Luz Towns-Miranda and Luis A. Miranda Jr., were both from Puerto Rico. Puerto Rico is a part of the United States, but it is not a state. Lin-Manuel grew up in a mostly Hispanic neighborhood. His home was full of music. Lin-Manuel started learning to play piano when he was six. His parents listened to Spanish songs and Broadway show tunes. His older sister, also named Luz, liked hip-hop.

"You'd hear all kinds of different music coming out of car windows and storefronts and fire escapes," Lin-Manuel said about his neighborhood. He gives his sister, Luz, the credit for his good taste in music. "All of my first hip-hop albums were stolen from her." She also helped him get ready for the very first time he was on stage—at the kindergarten talent show. (He sang a song, of course!)

Lin-Manuel's parents worked very hard, but the family didn't have money to see Broadway shows. They bought the cast albums instead. Lin-Manuel would listen to them over and over to memorize the lyrics. He also loved Disney movies like *Beauty and the Beast* and *The Lion King*.

Lin-Manuel's favorite film was *The Little Mermaid*, and he loved the funny crab character named Sebastian. He went to see the movie many times. In the fourth grade, he used to jump up on his desk at school and sing Sebastian's song "Under the Sea." He also memorized the dance moves. The Disney movies even inspired Lin-Manuel to make his own recordings and videos.

Lin-Manuel went to a school for gifted children in New York City. A school for gifted children is a school for extraordinarily smart kids. Lin-Manuel has talked about how happy he was to share Puerto Rican culture with his classmates. He shared exciting Latin music and delicious food.

Even though he was very smart, Lin-Manuel was still a bit intimidated by his classmates. He felt like they were all smarter than he was. So he decided to pick something he wanted to do and work really hard at it. That was singing, acting, and writing songs. By the sixth grade, he was in all the school musicals.

In high school, Lin-Manuel was in almost every school play. He wrote plays and musicals of his own, which showed his classmates what it was like to be Puerto Rican.

Lin-Manuel felt he had two choices. He could try to blend in, or he could try to stand out. He decided to stand out and make sure everyone knew he loved his Latino background.

Lin-Manuel also directed the show *West Side Story* in his senior year. The musical is about Puerto Rican and white teenagers in New York City who fight when a white boy falls in love with a Puerto Rican girl.

It wasn't just being Latino that made Lin-Manuel stand out. Everyone could see how talented he was. When it was time to go to college, he knew he would study musical theater. Lin-Manuel had a lot of dreams, but working in musical theater was the thing he most wanted to do.

Chapter 2
In the Heights

Lin-Manuel went to Wesleyan University in Connecticut to study theater arts. He performed in college musicals and wrote his own songs and shows. One of those shows was set in a Hispanic neighborhood near the one where Lin-Manuel grew up in New York City—Washington Heights. When he graduated college, he had a first draft of a musical called *In the Heights*. The show used Latin music and hip-hop to tell a story about the joys and troubles of the people in the neighborhood.

One week after he graduated from college, Lin-Manuel met with a friend from Wesleyan, Tommy Kail. Tommy was a theater director and thought *In the Heights* had promise. He encouraged Lin-Manuel to keep working on it and helped where he could. Other friends wanted them to meet a musician named Alex Lacamoire, who ended up joining them as the show's musical director.

While they were working on *In the Heights*, Lin-Manuel and Tommy also sang and acted with a hip-hop comedy group he had started in college called Freestyle Love Supreme. Audience members would shout out words, and Lin-Manuel and his friends would make up funny songs and skits. He wrote songs and acted in shows like *Sesame Street* and *The Electric Company*, and he also worked as a substitute teacher.

With Tommy as director, Alex as musical director, and Lin-Manuel in the lead role, *In the Heights* opened in a theater off-Broadway in 2007. Off-Broadway theaters are usually smaller than Broadway theaters.

In the Heights was a hit and moved to Broadway in 2008. It went on to win the Tony Award—the highest award a Broadway show can win—for Best Musical of the year. The cast recording won a Grammy Award.

Lin-Manuel's Broadway dreams were coming true. He continued to work on other shows, including a Spanish/English version of *West Side Story*, while he wondered what his next big project would be. Then one day he bought a biography of one of the United States founding fathers to read while he was on vacation. That biography of Alexander Hamilton would change his life.

Chapter 3
Hamilton's Beginnings

Lin-Manuel read about Alexander Hamilton's life while sitting by the pool at a hotel in Mexico. After just a few chapters, he realized that Hamilton would make a great subject for for a music album. Hamilton was a poor orphan from an island who came to America by himself. Hamilton then went on to become George Washington's right-hand man and a leader in the new country.

Lin-Manuel could relate to the story because his parents were poor and also came to the mainland U.S.

Lin-Manuel thought that hip-hop was the perfect music to tell Hamilton's story. Hip-hop music is filled with energy and excitement. So were the thirteen American colonies and the people who fought for independence from England.

Lin-Manuel had finished one song about Hamilton when he was invited to perform at the White House on May 12, 2009. President Barack Obama asked Lin-Manuel to sing a song from *In the Heights*, which was still on Broadway. Instead, Lin-Manuel decided to take a chance and try something

new. With Alex Lacamoire on the piano, Lin-Manuel sang about a poor immigrant who helped make America rich and strong. He sang "Alexander Hamilton," the song that would later be the opening number of the Broadway show.

The audience loved the song. President Obama was the first one on his feet to cheer. Millions of people watched Lin-Manuel sing the song on YouTube. Suddenly, the world wanted to know more about Alexander Hamilton—both the man and the album Lin-Manuel was working on.

For the next two years, Lin-Manuel was busy with other projects. Then, in June 2011, he sang "My Shot," the third song from the show, at a benefit performance. It had taken him more than a year to get the song exactly right.

The audience loved it. It was time for Lin-Manuel to get busy and write more songs.

Chapter 4
Broadway Bound

During the next three years, Lin-Manuel worked on *Hamilton* whenever he could. He also married Vanessa Nadal, a scientist and a lawyer. He first met Vanessa in high school. Lin-Manuel was too shy to talk to her then, but he found her on Facebook after college. He invited her to a Freestyle Love Supreme show and Vanessa went. Lin-Manuel was still too shy to talk to her that night, but a friend got her phone number for him. Vanessa came to more shows, and they started dating. They were married in 2010.

Vanessa and Lin-Manuel adopted a stray dog they found on a beach in the Dominican Republic. The half-starved dog nibbled on Vanessa's ankle. They decided to take the dog home and named her Tobillo, which is Spanish for "ankle." Today, they have two sons, Sebastian and Francisco. One of the reasons they named their first son Sebastian was because of the funny crab from *The Little Mermaid*!

All along, even after Lin-Manuel got
married, he was still working on *Hamilton*.
With the help of friends like Tommy and
Alex, the show was ready to open at an
off-Broadway theater in January 2015.
Lin-Manuel played Alexander Hamilton.

Some people were surprised that Lin-Manuel chose people of color to play many of the leading roles. Historically, the people the roles were based on had been white. But Lin-Manuel thought it was important for the cast to look like America today, not the America of two hundred years ago. He also wanted to celebrate the people of color who helped build the United States and didn't get credit in history books.

The show ended up being a huge success off-Broadway and moved to Broadway in July 2015, to the same theater where *In the Heights* played. (The theater is almost directly across the Hudson River from the spot where, in real life, Alexander Hamilton was shot by Aaron Burr in a duel in 1804.)

Hamilton was greeted by fireworks over the Hudson on opening night. It won the Pulitzer Prize for Drama and won eleven Tony Awards, including Best Musical. Lin-Manuel's friends Tommy and Alex also won Tony awards.

In July 2016, Lin-Manuel made his final appearance in the show. But *Hamilton* continues to break records on Broadway and beyond with shows opening in other cities around the country and even in London, England.

Chapter 5
Reaching New Heights

Lin-Manuel may have left the cast of *Hamilton*, but he hasn't stopped singing, acting, and writing songs. He wrote songs for the Disney film *Moana*. He has a starring role in the film *Mary Poppins Returns*. And he'll be working on the music for a live-action version of *The Little Mermaid*.

He continues to do everything he can to celebrate Latino culture and share that with the world. He also helps raise money for Puerto Rico and for important causes like women's health.

What else is in store for one of Broadway's most popular stars ever? Whatever it is, we know that Lin-Manuel will change the world with his art. He'll turn to his friends for help and work hard to make his dreams come true.

Now that you've met him, don't you think you can do the same?

BUT WAIT . . .

THERE'S MORE!

Turn the page to read a time line about Puerto Rico, discover some interesting facts about Broadway, and learn how to write your own play!

History of Puerto Rico

Lin-Manuel Miranda's family is from Puerto Rico, an island in the Caribbean Sea. Read this time line to learn about major events in Puerto Rico's history!

1000 C.E.: The Taino people live in Puerto Rico, which they call Boriquén. They eat cassava, which is a tropical root plant. They also eat sweet potatoes and seafood.

November 19, 1493: Christopher Columbus lands on the island and claims it for the Spanish king and queen.

1521: The Spanish explorer Ponce de León establishes a harbor named Puerto Rico, or "Rich Port." Over time, the name of the harbor changes to San Juan. The entire island becomes known as Puerto Rico.

1600s: San Juan becomes a military post for the Spanish army. The native people earn money by trading sugarcane, ginger, and cattle.

December 10, 1898: Spain loses the Spanish-American War and gives Puerto Rico to the United States. Puerto Ricans become U.S. citizens, but they aren't allowed to vote or choose their leaders.

October 1950: U.S. President Harry Truman signs the Puerto Rico Commonwealth Bill, which allows Puerto Ricans to have their own constitution and elect their own governor.

Today: Puerto Rico is still a commonwealth, but some people want it to become the fifty-first state of America. Others want Puerto Rico to become its own country.

Broadway by the Numbers

Become a Broadway theater expert with
these fun facts and figures.

• Broadway is a group of forty theaters in New York
that are mainly used for plays and musicals. A play is a
performance that tells the story through speech. A musical
tells the story through both singing and talking.

• Broadway shows usually have
eight performances each week.

• Only five theaters are actually
located on the street named
Broadway! The bulk of the
theaters are located on side
streets that cross Broadway.

• In the 2016–2017 season, people went to a Broadway
show thirteen million times.

• The longest running Broadway show is *The Phantom of the Opera*.

• The Tony Awards are like the Oscars for Broadway. There are twenty-six award categories, including "Best Costume Design of a Play" and "Best Direction of a Musical."

• *Hamilton* holds the record for the most Tony nominations ever—sixteen.

• *West Side Story* has been produced five different times on Broadway. Lin-Manuel Miranda worked on the fifth production. The show has also toured America two times.

Write Your Own Play

Write your own play script by following these simple steps. Maybe someday you, too, will become a Broadway writer!

First brainstorm **ideas** about the story of the play. Do you want it to be nonfiction (a story that took place in real life) or fiction (something you make up yourself)? Will it be funny, spooky, sad, or happy? Where should it take place?

Next it's time to think about the **characters**. Are they human or not? How do the characters know one another? If you're stuck, try reading biographies of famous people—that's how Lin-Manuel decided to write *Hamilton*!

Just like this book has chapters, or parts, a play can be divided into different **scenes**. How many scenes do you want your play to have?

Now you're ready to write. Plays are made up of **dialogue** and **stage directions**. Dialogue, or speaking lines, are the words that the characters say out loud. Stage directions are included

for the actors and actresses. They describe an action, a character's feelings, or any other important information. The dialogue and stage directions are written in this style.

LIN-MANUEL
(pointing off stage)
Look at that dog!

(TOBILLO approaches VANESSA,
sniffing her feet.)

VANESSA
Where is the owner?

LIN-MANUEL
(worried)
Maybe she's a stray dog. She looks really
hungry.

VANESSA
(laughing)
She's hungry enough to try
to eat my ankle!

Those are all the basics you need for writing a play. If you
want to make a musical like Lin-Manuel Miranda did, you can
include song lyrics in your play too. Don't forget to add a title.
Congratulations—now you're a playwright!

Now that you've met Lin-Manuel, what have you learned?

1. Where were Lin-Manuel's parents born?

a. Puerto Rico   b. Florida   c. New York

2. According to Lin-Manuel, who helped him gain good taste in music?

a. his mom   b. his sister   c. his drama teacher

3. When Lin-Manuel was younger, how did he memorize song lyrics?

a. He wrote the lyrics down.

b. He listened to the songs many times.

c. He made dance moves to the songs.

4. What languages does Lin-Manuel speak?

a. English and Spanish   b. English and Hindi   c. English and Latin

5. What show did Lin-Manuel write in college?

a. *The Electric Company*   b. *In the Heights*   c. *Washington's Story*

6. What is the name of Lin-Manuel's freestyle rap group?

a. Alexander Hamilton   b. Rapping for All   c. Freestyle Love Supreme

7. Why did Lin-Manuel choose hip-hop for *Hamilton*?

a. He thought Broadway music was boring.

b. Hip-hop is energetic and exciting.

c. Alexander Hamilton liked hip-hop.

8. What happened after Lin-Manuel sang at the White House?

a. Lin-Manuel appeared on *Sesame Street*.

b. President Obama asked for an autograph.

c. Everyone watched the video on YouTube.

9. Why is Lin-Manuel's dog named Tobillo?

a. The dog nibbled Vanessa's ankle, and Tobillo means "ankle" in Spanish.

b. Tobillo means "dog" in Spanish.

c. It rhymes with Lin-Manuel's middle name.

10. What is NOT a reason why Lin-Manuel chose actors and actresses of color for *Hamilton*?

a. He wanted to work with the same cast as *In the Heights*.

b. He wanted the cast to look like America today.

c. He wanted to celebrate the people who get left out of history books.

Answers: 1.a 2.b 3.b 4.a 5.b 6.c 7.b 8.c 9.a 10.a

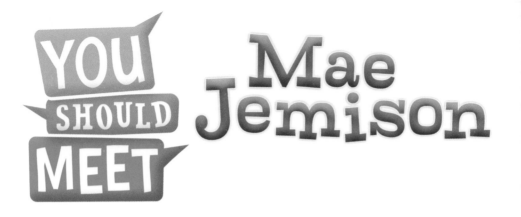

YOU SHOULD MEET

Mae Jemison

by Laurie Calkhoven
illustrated by Monique Dong

Ready-to-Read

Simon Spotlight
New York   London   Toronto   Sydney   New Delhi

CONTENTS

Have you ever looked up at the stars and wanted to fly? Have you dreamed of being an astronaut and blasting off into space? Or of being a dancer? Or being a doctor who brings medical care to people around the world?

If you've ever dreamed of any of those things, then you should meet Mae Jemison!

Mae is the first African American woman to become an astronaut. But she's much more than that. Mae is also . . .

a **scientist**

and **a dancer.**

And she's **a doctor, an author,**

and **a teacher.**

Today she's working to find ways for humans to travel beyond our solar system. Mae followed her dreams . . . all of them. Once you meet her, you'll know you can follow yours too!

Chapter 1
Early Dreams

Mae was born in Decatur, Alabama, on October 17, 1956. She has two older siblings, a sister and a brother. Her father was a carpenter and her mother taught elementary school.

When Mae was three years old, her family moved from Alabama to Chicago, Illinois. She thinks of Chicago as her hometown.

Mae always loved science. When her kindergarten teacher asked her what she wanted to be when she grew up, Mae said, "a scientist." Many people at the time didn't think it was possible for an African American girl to become a scientist. Women were more likely to become teachers and nurses than scientists.

"Don't you mean a nurse?" the teacher asked.

"No, I mean a **scientist**," Mae answered.

Other teachers tried to discourage Mae too. She wouldn't let them. She never stopped believing in herself. She stood strong in the face of other people's questions.

At home Mae was encouraged to be anything she wanted to be. "My parents were the best scientists I knew, because they were always asking questions," she said when she was grown up.

Mae considered herself a "busybody" and liked to get involved with her sister's and brother's science projects.

Once, she got a splinter in her thumb. Soon there was pus. Other kids might have been grossed out and just wanted it to go away, but not Mae. Mae wanted to know exactly what the pus was and where it came from. So she did a scientific study of pus to learn about how it fights infection to help our bodies heal.

Mae's family talked about many things around the dinner table, including the civil rights movement. The civil rights movement was a mass popular movement to secure equal access to and opportunities for the basic privileges and rights of US citizenship for African Americans. There were sometimes riots, and one time, National Guard soldiers came to Chicago to keep the peace. Mae was scared, but she promised herself that she wouldn't let fear keep her from doing what she wanted in the world.

The library was a place where Mae learned about science. She read all kinds of science books, especially ones about the stars.

Mae also followed the National Aeronautics and Space Administrations (NASA) space programs in the newspapers. She knew all about the astronauts and their missions.

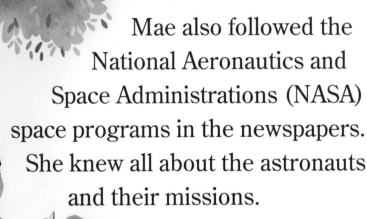

"Growing up, I always assumed I would go into space," Mae said when she was older. "I remember being really, really irritated that there were no women astronauts."

Mae was inspired by the character Uhura, a female officer on the television show Star Trek. Uhura was played by the actress Nichelle Nichols. Eventually Mae got to meet Nichelle.

Mae believes that the best scientists are not only logical but creative too. She took all kinds of dance lessons growing up—ballet, jazz, modern, African, and even Japanese dancing. She wanted to be a professional dancer. She also designed and made clothes for her dolls, acted in school plays, and took art classes.

But science was always Mae's first love. She graduated high school at sixteen and won a scholarship to Stanford University to study engineering.

Chapter 2
Dreams on Earth

At Stanford University in California, Mae majored in chemical engineering. Biochemical engineering was her focus. A biochemical engineer creates things to make medical care better. Mae also majored in African and Afro-American history. And just like she had when she was younger, Mae combined art and creativity with science.

Mae created dance routines, acted in plays, and was president of the Black Student Union. She also learned to speak Swahili, an African language.

In college Mae decided that she wanted to be a medical doctor. When she graduated from Stanford, she moved to New York City to go to Cornell University Medical College. Mae studied hard, but she also made time for fun. She took dance lessons, and she went to the theater with friends.

During her summer breaks, Mae traveled to Kenya and Cuba to learn about medical care in other countries, especially for poor people.

She also worked in Thailand at a camp for *refugees*—people who had been driven away from their homes by war.

At first, Mae didn't want to be the kind of doctor who sees patients. She wanted to be the kind of doctor who does research. But working in other countries made her interested in bringing medicine to people in poor areas around the world.

After she became a doctor, Mae volunteered for the Peace Corps.

The Peace Corps is made up of Americans who bring things such as medical care, clean water, and education to people in underdeveloped countries. As a doctor for the Peace Corps, Mae went to Sierra Leone and Liberia, two countries in West Africa.

After two and a half years in Africa, Mae returned to California to work as a doctor. It was then that she remembered an early dream—a dream to fly into space.

She learned that NASA was accepting applications for the astronaut program, so Mae applied.

People who want to be astronauts must have college degrees in science, math, or engineering. They also need to have work experience in their fields and show NASA that they can be leaders.

Mae's application stood out. NASA asked her to travel to the Johnson Space Center in Houston, Texas, for interviews and physical tests. Mae must have shown them how smart and strong she was, because in June 1987 NASA asked her to be an astronaut candidate. She was one of fifteen chosen out of a group of two thousand people.

Mae's early dream was coming true. She was on her way to becoming an astronaut!

Chapter 3
Dreams about Space

Mae was chosen by NASA in 1987, but she wasn't an astronaut yet. She was an "astronaut *candidate*." A candidate is someone who is applying for a particular job. Astronaut candidates have to take classes and work hard to learn new things before they are given the title "astronaut."

One thing Mae had to learn before she could go into space was what it was like to be weightless. Astronauts call this *microgravity*. Gravity is the force that keeps humans—and everything else— from floating off Earth and into space. But in space you feel only a tiny amount of gravity's pull.

Astronauts need to be able to do their jobs while they are weightless. One way they learn how to do that is by flying in a special airplane. The plane makes many people sick to their stomachs.

The plane's nickname is the Vomit Comet!

Mae also needed to learn how to survive in the wilderness and in the water. That was in case her spaceship landed in the wrong place when it came back to Earth.

After a year of hard training, Mae was finally named an astronaut!

Not all astronauts fly into space. Many work on Earth, helping the astronauts who are in space. At first Mae worked as

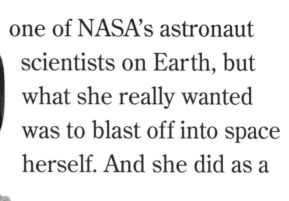

one of NASA's astronaut scientists on Earth, but what she really wanted was to blast off into space herself. And she did as a

Science Mission Specialist.

Science mission specialists perform experiments, among many other jobs, in space.

Chapter 4
Space!

On September 12, 1992, Mae became the first African American woman to travel into space.

The first white American woman to fly into space, Sally Ride, had done so in June 1983. The first African American male astronaut, Guion Bluford, had gone into space two months later in August 1983. Now Mae was making history by being both a woman and an African American.

Mae flew on the space shuttle *Endeavour.* She spent about eight days in space and completed almost 127 orbits of the Earth. In that time she traveled more than three million miles!

Mae wanted to celebrate art and creativity in space. Among other items, she brought a poster of an African American dancer and a statue made by a women's group in West Africa onto the shuttle.

In orbit, the astronauts did experiments. Mae wanted to know why some people get sick to their stomachs in space and how to make them feel better.

Mae also wanted to learn about how tadpoles grew when they were weightless. Mae discovered tadpoles grew just like they do in Earth's gravity.

"When we got back to Earth, the tadpoles were right on track," Mae told a reporter after her mission. The tadpoles later turned into frogs, just like they were supposed to.

Mae was never afraid in space. "I was very excited and happy," she said. She remembered being a young girl who loved to stare up at the stars.

"The first thing I saw from space was Chicago, my hometown. . . . Looking out the window of that space shuttle, I thought if that little girl growing up in Chicago could see her older self now, she would have a huge grin on her face."

The flight made Mae famous. She realized she could use her fame to talk about how important it is to take care of the planet. She also wanted people of all races to know they could be part of the scientific world.

Chapter 5
Life after Space

After flying into space, Mae decided to leave NASA and do other things. She became a college professor. She started a company that brings technology and better medical care to people in poor countries. She also became an actress when she appeared on the TV show *Star Trek: The Next Generation. Star Trek* was one of Mae's favorite TV shows when she was young.

Getting kids involved in science was also something Mae wanted to do. She started a camp for students who want to become scientists. The camp, called The Earth We Share, welcomes young scientists from all over the world.

These campers get to do more than hike or sleep in a tent. They use their imaginations and plan amazing things—such as a space mission to Mars!

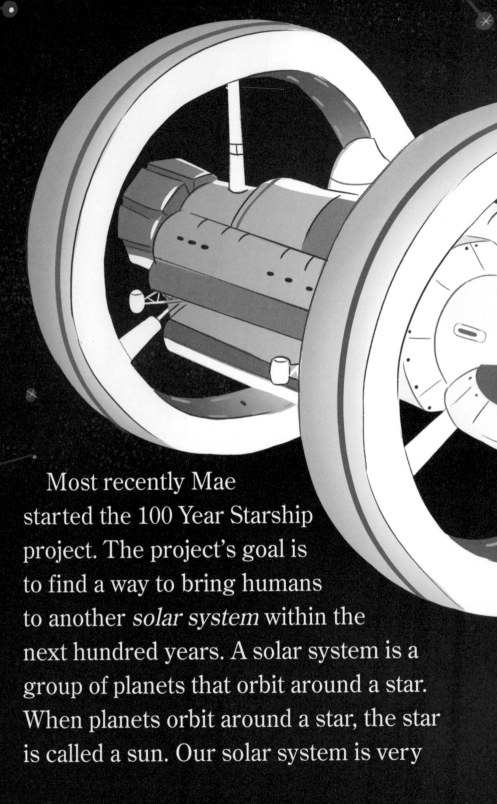

Most recently Mae
started the 100 Year Starship
project. The project's goal is
to find a way to bring humans
to another *solar system* within the
next hundred years. A solar system is a
group of planets that orbit around a star.
When planets orbit around a star, the star
is called a sun. Our solar system is very

far away from any other solar system.

Today it would take us seventy thousand years to travel to another solar system! The 100 Year Starship program will have to create everything from new kinds of energy to new kinds of filters that will keep air and water clean. A starship might need a garden for fresh fruits and vegetables, and things to help the astronauts survive on a new planet.

Most of all, Mae wants to make sure that all kinds of people, not just Americans and not just doctors, will have a chance to be involved.

Mae always believed in following her dreams, and she never let people tell her she couldn't. She also refused to become any one thing—a scientist or an artist, a doctor or a dancer. Mae believed she could do anything, and she did!

Now that you've met Mae Jemison, don't you think you can do the same thing? Reach for the stars—and more!

BUT WAIT...

THERE'S MORE!

Turn the page to try a science experiment similar to the ones Mae did in space, to read how Mae saved a life, and to read some facts about Mae's mission on board the space shuttle *Endeavour*.

Life Sciences Experiment

Aboard the space shuttle *Endeavour*, Mae did experiments to study how living things would react to being in space.

You can do experiments like Mae without even leaving your house! Follow the directions below to discover how plants react to three different environments.

Materials

3 plastic sandwich bags
12 dry pinto beans
3 paper towels
Water
Stapler with staples
Tape
Ruler
A journal or other place to write notes
A grown-up to help with the stapler

Step 1: Fold each paper towel into fourths so that it will fit into a sandwich bag.

Step 2: Put one folded paper towel into each bag.

Step 3: For each bag, staple four times through the paper towel, from right to left, about an inch from the bottom. Space out the staples evenly and make sure they are going straight across, not up and down.

Step 4: Inside the bag, place one bean on top of each staple.

Step 5: Find three different places to grow your beans, and tape one bag at each spot. Make sure each area has a different environment—someplace sunny, someplace shady, and someplace dark. Try taping one bag to a window, one to a wall beside a window, and another to the inside of a cabinet.

Step 6: Water your beans by pouring half an inch of water into each bag. Make sure the water doesn't rise above the staples.

Step 7: After about five days, you should see small green shoots sprouting from some of the beans.

Step 8: Keep watering your beans with half an inch of water once a week. Every time you water your plants, use the ruler to measure how long the shoots are, and then write down your findings. After a couple of weeks, you will start to notice a difference in the way the beans are growing.

Step 9: After two weeks, look at the measurements you've taken. Can you come to any conclusions about the way each environment affected the beans? Write your conclusions down.

Step 10: Now that you've made a discovery, share the results!

WHAT IT MEANS
This experiment studies how beans react to the amount of sunlight in their environment. You can study how beans react to other environments by changing the experiment. Make sure there is only one thing different about each environment for the beans. Otherwise, you won't know which change has affected the way they grow.

You can also experiment with:
• Different amounts of water.
• Different types of water, like salt water or sugar water.
• Different sources of light, like fluorescent or colored lightbulbs.
• Different temperatures.

Mae to the Rescue!

When Mae first became a doctor, she traveled to Sierra Leone in West Africa. She volunteered her medical services through the Peace Corps. Within two weeks one of the Peace Corps volunteers became very sick.

The other doctors thought the volunteer had malaria. Malaria is a disease that can cause a high fever, muscle pain, and vomiting. It is common in tropical climates like that of Sierra Leone. People can die of malaria if they are not treated. After receiving treatment for one day, the volunteer was worse. Mae knew that he did not have malaria. If he did not receive a different treatment, he would die.

Soon after the electricity went out at the hospital. Mae used a flashlight to search for medicine to give the volunteer a different treatment. Even if she found the medicine, it would not cure him completely. Mae was sure he was sick with meningitis. Meningitis is an illness that will kill a person if not treated correctly, and no one had the correct treatment nearby.

Mae ordered a military medical evacuation. That meant a plane would take the volunteer to an air force hospital for treatment. Mae was a new doctor, and she was giving an order that would cost more than eighty thousand dollars. The people at the US embassy did not think she could give such a big order.

Mae did not give up. She calmly explained that she had the power to give the order, and she clarified why it was absolutely necessary. She refused to take no for an answer—a man's life was at stake. The people at the embassy finally listened to her, and Mae evacuated with the volunteer. In all, she worked for fifty-six hours straight to save the man's life.

Thanks to Mae's self-confidence and brave decisions, the volunteer survived.

Mae's Mission by the Numbers

- Mae went into space on a mission called STS-47. It was the second flight of twenty-five for the space shuttle *Endeavour.*

- The mission lasted seven days, twenty-two hours, thirty minutes, twenty-three seconds from blast off to touchdown.

- The mission launched on September 12, 1992 at 10:23:00 a.m. Eastern Daylight Time and landed on September 20, 1992 at 8:53:23 a.m. Eastern Daylight Time.

- When the shuttle launched, it weighed 258,679 pounds. That's more than twenty-five school buses! When the shuttle landed, it weighed 218,854 pounds, having lost 39,825 pounds. Fuel, an external tank, and two solid rocket motors were either used up or ejected during the mission.

- The shuttle orbited Earth at an altitude, or height, of about 191 miles. That's about thirty-five times higher than the peak of Mount Everest.

• The shuttle orbited earth about 127 times, traveling 3.3 million miles. (That's close to the distance you'd travel to go to the moon and back seven times.)

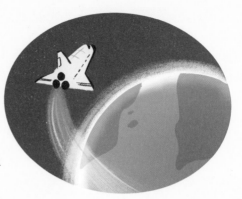

• There were seven crew members.

• The STS-47 mission included three firsts: the first Japanese astronaut to fly aboard the shuttle, payload specialist Mamoru Mohri; the first African American woman to fly in space, mission specialist Mae Jemison; and the first married couple to fly on the same space expedition, mission specialists Mark C. Lee and N. Jan Davis.

Now that you've met Mae, what do you know about her?

1. What year was Mae born?

a. 1956   b. 1960   c. 1972

2. Mae believes that the best scientists are what?

a. Quiet   b. Curious   c. Stubborn

3. According to Mae, why were her parents the best scientists she knew?

a. They studied.   b. They day dreamed.   c. They asked questions.

4. Mae always knew she would do something specific. What was that?

a. Go to space   b. Be a leader   c. Study tadpoles

5. Besides science, what were some of Mae's interests?

a. Art and dance   b. Geography and history   c. Math and magic

6. When Mae finished medical school, what did she do next?

a. Started an organization   b. Joined the Peace Corps   c. Joined NASA

7. On September 12, 1992, Mae became the first ___ in space?

a. Woman   b. Doctor   c. African American
woman

8. What did Mae do in space?

a. Conducted experiments   b. Built robots   c. Studied Earth

9. How did Mae feel in space?

a. Excited and afraid   b. Sick but happy   c. Excited and happy

10. After going to space, what did Mae want to do?

a. Help people and encourage space exploration.

b. Become a dancer and a writer.   c. Go on a mission to the sun.

Answers: 1.a 2.b 3.c 4.a 5.a 6.b 7.c 8.a 9.c 10.a

REPRODUCIBLE